DC SUPER-VILLAINS
THE OFFICIAL COLOURING BOOK

TITAN BOOKS

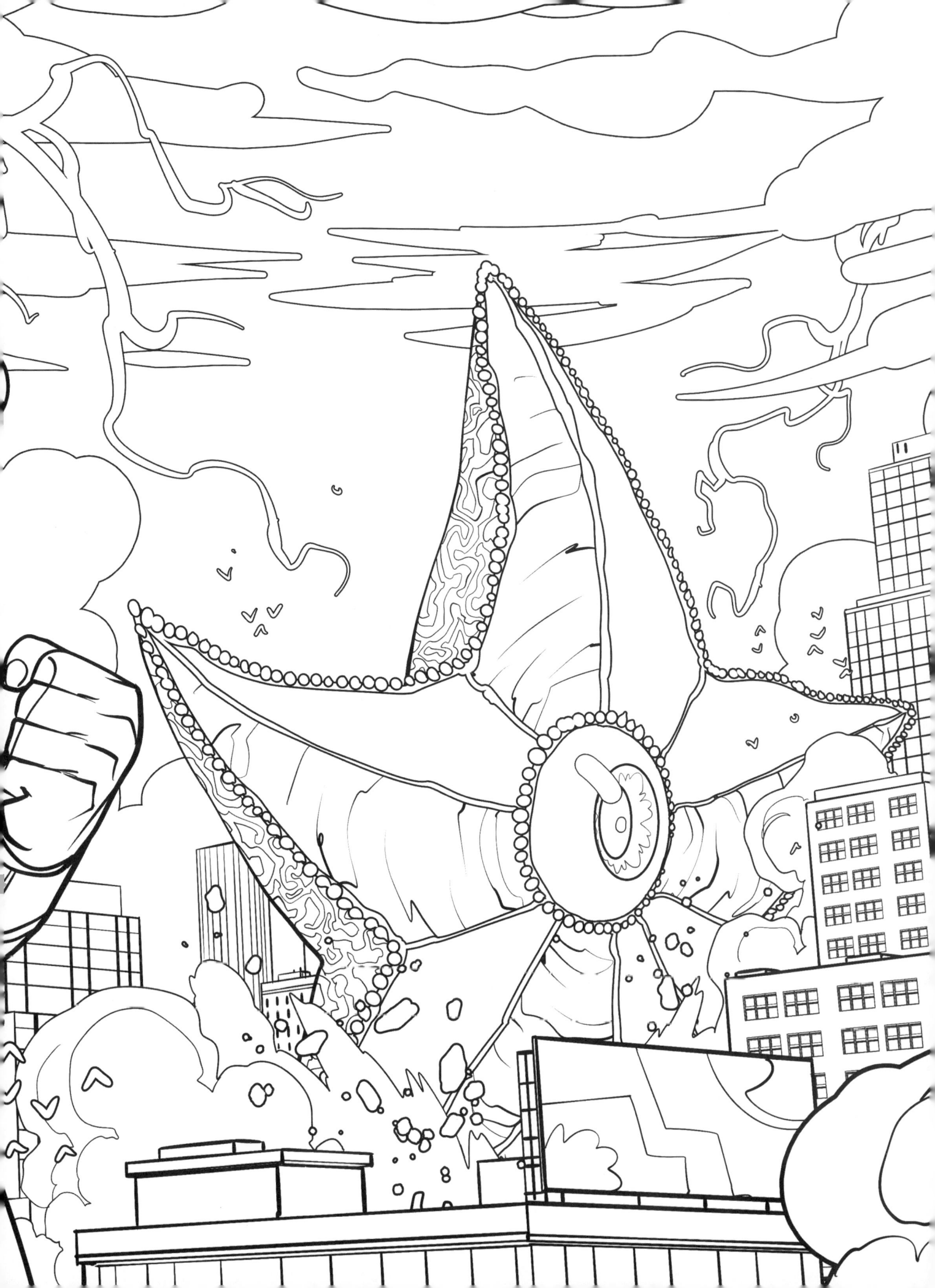

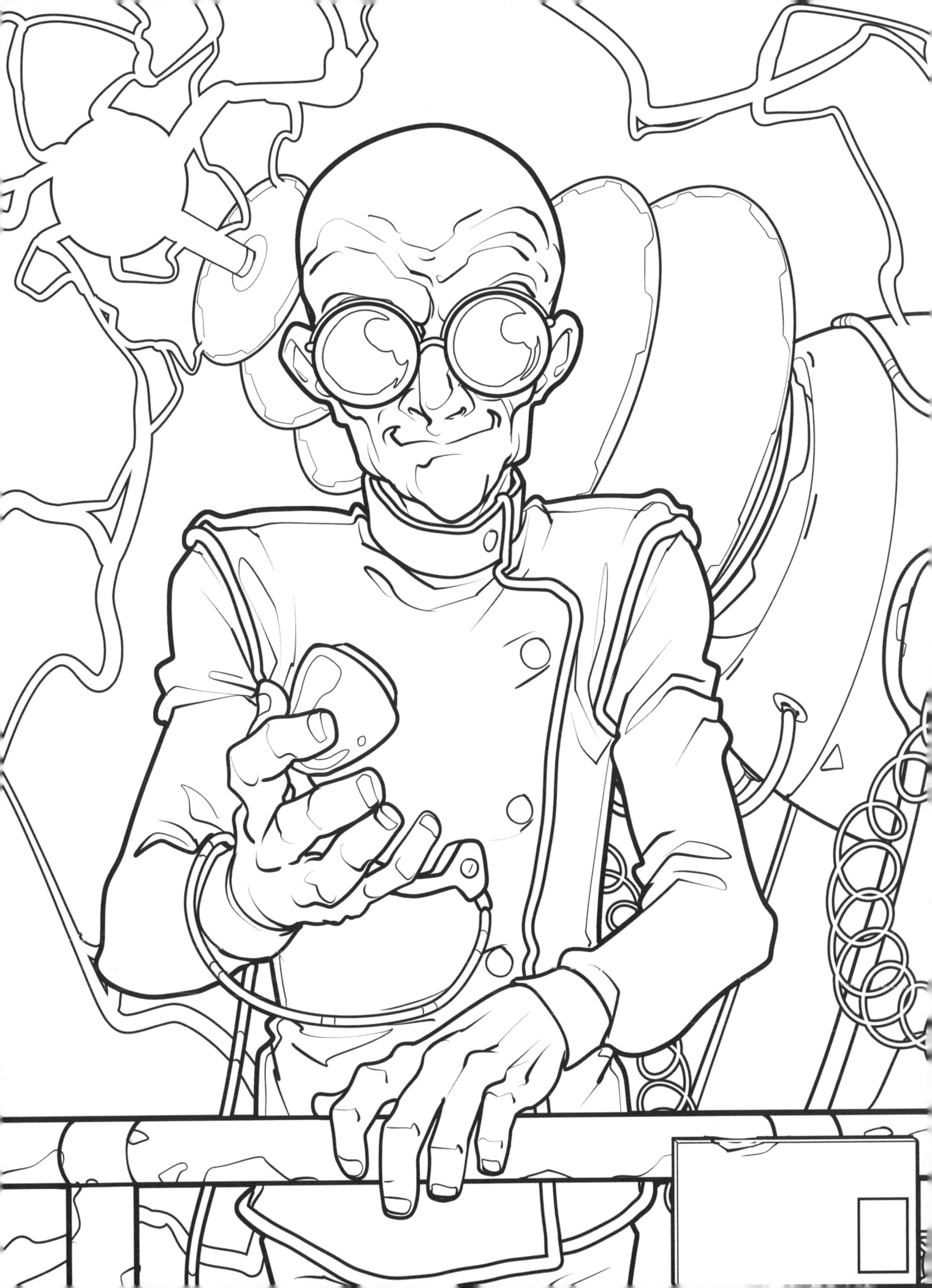

TITAN BOOKS

Published by Titan Books, London, in 2023
A division of Titan Publishing Group Ltd
144 Southwark Street
London SE1 0UP
www.titanbooks.com

 Find us on Facebook: facebook.com/TitanBooks
 Follow us on Twitter: @TitanBooks

 Copyright © 2023 DC.
All DC characters and elements © & ™ DC.
WB Shield ™ & © WBEI. (s23)

Superman created by Jerry Siegel and Joe Shuster.
By special arrangement with the Jerry Siegel family.

Published by Titan Books, London, in 2023.

No part of this publication may be reproduced, stored in a retrieval system, or transmitted, in any form or by any means without the prior written permission of the publisher, nor be otherwise circulated in any form of binding or cover other than that in which it is published and without a similar condition being imposed on the subsequent purchase.

A CIP catalogue record for this title is available from the British Library.

ISBN: 9781803367002

Publisher: Raoul Goff
VP, Co-Publisher: Vanessa Lopez
VP, Creative: Chrissy Kwasnik
VP, Manufacturing: Alix Nicholaeff
VP, Group Managing Editor: Vicki Jaeger
Publishing Director: Jamie Thompson
Design Manager: Megan Sinead Bingham
Senior Editor: Justin Eisinger
Editorial Assistant: Sami Alvarado
Managing Editor: Maria Spano
Senior Production Editor: Michael Hylton
Production Associate: Tiffani Patterson
Senior Production Manager, Subsidiary Rights: Lina s Palma-Temena

Illustrations by José Carlos Silva

Insight Editions, in association with Roots of Peace, will plant two trees for each tree used in the manufacturing of this book. Roots of Peace is an internationally renowned humanitarian organization dedicated to eradicating land mines worldwide and converting war-torn lands into productive farms and wildlife habitats. Roots of Peace will plant two million fruit and nut trees in Afghanistan and provide farmers there with the skills and support necessary for sustainable land use.

Manufactured in China by Insight Editions

10 9 8 7 6 5 4 3 2 1